Revealed by Kali, channelised by Ekta

1. Introduction - page 8
2. Circle of healing - page 11
3. *Empowerment (Initiation) - page 15*
4. The empowered warrior woman - page 17
5. Knowing your Kali - page 22
6. The inner warrior - page 23
7. Words to evoke your inner warrior - page 24
8. Age of Kali and her message for women - page 25
9. *Knowledge (Preparation) - page 29*
10. The spirit of lotus - page 31
11. Cleansing the soul - page 32
12. Living without fear - page 33
13. *Truth (Acceptance) - page 35*
14. Dreams are messages from another dimension - page 37
15. Discovering your truth - page 40
16. Follow your calling - page 41
17. *Awakening (Realisation) - page 43*
18. The awakened woman - page 45
19. The candle of curiosity - page 48
20. Befriending the darkness - page 50
21. *Wisdom (Nurture) - page 53*
22. Kali and Buddha - page 55
23. The void of wisdom - page 58
24. Breaking the spiral - page 60

25. *Love (Healing) - page 63*
26. Melody of a soul - page 65
27. Merging in absolute love - page 66
28. Expanding the grace - page 69
29. *Patience (Reflecting) - page 71*
30. The subtle changes - page 73
31. Potent power of silence - page 75
32. Feminine grace - page 76
33. *Grace (Receiving) - page 79*
34. Beauty of a woman - page 81
35. The mandala of life - page 82
36. Understanding trust - page 83
33. *Surrender (Knowing) - page 85*
34. Polarities of life - page 87
35. Spiritual dancers of the same tribe - page 88
36. A novel view of self - page 91
37. *Oneness (Merging) - page 93*
38. Finding the balance - page 95
39. Embracing relationships - page 97
40. Joining the tribe - page 101
41. *The Kali moment - page 103*
42. My Kali moment - page 107
43. A new beginning - page 113
44. Join my tribe - page 114

for my guru, Swami Vivekananda
for Vedanta

INTRODUCTION

Our energies are a combination of both; male and female dimension. *The Voice of Kali* focuses on the feminine energy within us. Every time I refer to 'women', I am referring to the feminine energy in all. I truly believe that women are naturally and innately empowered beings.

Have you ever seen a mother instantly transform into a gorilla state when her child is being attacked or is in danger? She needs no lesson in embracing empowerment. Her dormant Kali will instantly flare up when she needs to shield her family. Because women are also born out of perennial beauty of mesmerising spring, they are deeply connected to the personality traits of mother nature. This makes compassion, empathy, nurturing and discipline her natural state. When nature's imbalance is even slightly disturbed, it results in catastrophic disasters. The same air that helps us breathe can turn into tornadoes; the same fire that warms our house can burn in fury; the same water that relinquishes our thirst can drown in rage. This is the power of the mother nature that quietly nurtures and witnesses millions of lives repeatedly go through their karmic cycle.

This is also the power that is burning within every woman. She will lovingly nurture and closely watch her family evolve, but when her patience, love and compassion is tested to its limit, the dance of imbalance is unleashed, and from there, right from the ashes of humiliation and transformation, sprouts her inner Kali: the one who knows to protect fiercely, embrace compassionately, heal lovingly, love unconditionally and nurture carefully. Every woman has these archetypes within her. Kali, the warrior, encompasses all the archetypes. She will take the form of the energy that your soul is seeking and lovingly remind you that you have the power to rise from the ashes and completely transform your life.

CIRCLE OF HEALING

Although numerous treatises have been written in the glory of Kali, not many speak about her essence in the simplicity that it exists. Spiritual experiences must be understood in the psychic realm but within the physical realm; each experience must be dealt with the same childlike wonder and seen with the eye of naivety.

The journey comes to a pause the day one ceases to wonder what vibrates in the subtle movements of the mind, and likewise what exists in the silence when the movement stops. This inquisitiveness is the essence of knowledge. Its core lies in the centre of a timeless void; the space from where, with each experience, the dots start joining together to form the circle of awakening. With every new revelation, the circle comes closer to culmination, and depending on our choices, it gradually illuminates the truth of our existence. The journey goes on a timeless loop till the illusion of form is broken and the soul realises that there is no beginning, no end; the liberated energy then merges back to a void of higher dimension. This darkness, this void, is where the empowered energy of Kali vibrates and initiates the process of creation.

Energy, as we know, is neither created nor destroyed. It has neither the feminine nor the masculine form. Just as water takes the shape of its vessel, the energy takes the form it vibrates in. Since Kali is the beginning, she animates within all forms. Kali's essence, though, is that of the feminine warrior, which reflects that she will raise the psychic state of empowerment with compassion. The feminine form is the nurturer and the healer whose innate nature is to restore the initial destruction of illusion.

The energy of Kali initially awakens the masculine energy of power and aggression within us and concludes with the contradictory nurturing, reasoning and healing feminine energy. For those who need a trigger to break the illusion, she resonates the intensity of masculinity, and for those who need to open perception, she vibrates the feminine energy. This dance of destruction and nurturing goes on endlessly until the form merges in the void. It's imperative to know that energy resonates in the void too. Sometimes the fleeting vibrations of the higher dimension connect with a distant energy on the physical dimension – in the form of thoughts, intuitions, visions or dreams. Through this book, my ardent quest has been to demystify the myth that the psychic ability belongs only to the spiritually gifted; all souls are spiritual and gifted with absolute knowledge. We just have to learn to find our own individual circle of awakening. If we peruse carefully, we can see that there are patterns and secret codes within the depths of our soul, which, when illuminated, become our guiding light.

As a young girl, I was always scared of the persona of Kali. I could never quite comprehend the need for a goddess to look so fierce. Though my soul was drawn to her energy, my ignorance about her essence clouded my intuition. The universe had other plans, and it's only through her I understood the true nature of my soul. Her visionary messages and her aura have left mind expanding imprints in my consciousness. The bizarre way that energies of the revered master Swami Vivekananda and many more have opened the secret codes of life for me is overwhelming and magical. This book is, however, not about magic and miracle or mythology and culture. It's about the energy that I embraced through my spiritual journey and its power. I want women to know the power and love that the energy of Kali radiates. I wish for them to forget her form and just connect to her energy.

There is a surge in fear and uncertainty in the lives of people, but women, even under the chaotic circumstances, know how to hold on to hope. My aim for this book is to open the path of that small ray of hope and give tools to women for turning that tiny beam of light into a raging fire of wisdom, honour, love and courage. The need of the hour is to show women a way to illuminate the world through their energy, doing so with an optimum power and by making the right choices. They need to honour their intuition and their warrior archetype, their Kali.

We are nothing but vessels. Pour, don't store.

Initiation

EMPOWERMENT

Kali, become my voice, guide what I say,
She laughs merrily at my ignorant display.
Have you been the one to speak?
Are you the one to awaken the meek?
You are inviting me to my own abode.
I have travelled many times on that road.
Your form diminishes and decays,
My power is infinite, I rule the night and day.
I colour your soul red with passion and wisdom,
Merge in my madness, dance in my rhythm,
I was never away from your side,
You searched everywhere but never inside,
You are Kali, the lover and teacher,
You are Kali, the life in every creature,
You are Kali, the warrior in action and saint at heart,
You heal, you empower, you are the soul of every art.
Awaken the woman you always were,
No bondage of fear, no norms to concur,
Be Kali, the free spirit of divine,
My power is yours, let your pain be mine.

–Ekta

–Ekta

- EMPOWERMENT -

THE EMPOWERED WARRIOR WOMAN

Within every woman lives another woman waiting to be discovered. She will be revealed gradually. Sooner or later, one of these women will show up time and again in different circumstances. If you are a woman, you will know what I am saying. If you are a man, you must have at some point seen a glimpse of the mysterious woman masked behind the veils of your girl.

Either way, the encounter might have baffled you, clouding your mind with numerous questions. Who is she? Do I know her? She looks distant yet deeply intimate. You possess her heart but her spirit is free. The truth is, she is the essence that lives within each and every woman. This essence can be seen and felt even in little girls. What we perceive as mood swings are, in reality, a switch of energy in that little angel. She is gradually polishing her skills, discovering her uniqueness, and understanding that she has the natural ability to withstand every storm. She has an inner fire that will guide her to connect with complimenting energies. Her intuition, her dreams, her charms, her ways, her words, her world is different and this is something that every girl knows right from the time her mind has learnt to comprehend life. Now, as this little girl grows into a woman, this feeling of uniqueness will either elevate or alleviate. Depending on her choice of thoughts, she will either feed her soul with depth or doubt.

- EMPOWERMENT -

The girl could grow up totally unaware of her powers, losing the sight of them under the dust of social norms. There is also a possibility that maybe she keeps the little light within her burning, feeds it often with her belief and finally one day discovers the path that leads to the true light of her soul. No matter what your choices have been as you grew, you will at some point feel the trigger of light, bouts of latent power, shown glimpses of a shadow that follows your doubts, nudges of awakening and alienation from your outward masked self.

Your soul recognises the energy that is calling you but you are still not ready to embrace it. The energy will follow you constantly, compel you to question your choices, to dig deep within the open wounds, to sink seeds in the barren patches of your soul and explore your deepest, darkest thoughts. You might run, hide or ignore, but some day you will embrace that power and let it envelop you with its grace until you completely surrender and awaken to its glory. When that happens, and once you have done what she directs you to do, that's when in one instant you will realise that you are part of an infinite flame. You are the energy that you have been dodging; you are the truth that you have been searching for; you are the healer, the nurturer, the carer, the giver, the seductress and the lover. You are the life that dwells in the veins of the tiniest flower.

- EMPOWERMENT -

You are the strength of the mountains; you are the fighter, the Buddha, the warrior. You are Kali, the powerful, forgiving, enriching and encompassing warrior woman, Kali.

Kali is our inner voice, the truth within us. She brings forth what's authentic and banishes the fake. She dwells in passion and inspires us to work towards a better life with vigour. She manifests as energy and guides us to eliminate the darkness within us and around us. Kali is a force, a light that takes birth in our darkest times.

It's true that we women are much more scared of darkness than men. Have you ever wondered why? What is it about the dark that kindles the thought of an unknown presence in our minds? Every single sound, every movement, every breath becomes prominent in the depths of darkness. Think back to a time when you were in a dark room all by yourself. What did you feel? Were you suddenly aware of someone's presence? You probably frantically searched for the light switch to relieve the anxiety. Once that light was switched on, life felt normal again. You went back to singing, reading or simply merging yourself in the humdrum of life. But, clearly, that moment when you were in the dark was one of the few most intimate moments you have ever spent with yourself. It was a time when your conscious was aware of the sounds that otherwise bypass your ears. Your soul could sense the vibrations that are an intrinsic part of our universe. Your senses were heightened; you were aware of even the tiniest beam of light and were probably thankful for its presence for leading the way to the light switch. *This is what darkness does to a woman. It elevates her senses and brings her forth to an intrinsic sense of intuition.* She gradually adapts to morph into a fighter and a survivor. Darkness compels her to use her powers and gives her a glimpse of the warrior within her, something that the illusion of light conceals.

Try this when you are ready. Switch off the lights in your room at night. Gradually become aware of the sounds, the vibrations and the smell. These are not alien to you; they are the energies that you have played with all your life, sometimes through intuition and sometimes because of deep insight . Merge your fear in the darkness and let it guide you around the room. You will be amazed at how easily and powerfully you naturally command the dark. Tune into your soul power, your thoughts and your dreams. Take a deep breath and command the space you are in. Now, with confidence, walk towards the light switch and turn it on, not with fear but with dominance. Remember, one who conquers the dark commands

- EMPOWERMENT -

the light. It may be momentary, but you have evoked the Kali within you. These small little steps, small, tiny beams of lights, will gradually take you towards the infinite power and light that dwells within you. This analogy is not different to what women experience in their dark times. A feeling and sense of being lost is subtly replaced by a heightened sense of perception, cautiousness, comfort and understanding.

Her Kali guides her, soothes and empowers her to gradually rise to a new level of inner consciousness. Guided by her instincts, she befriends the dark times. Challenges become opportunities, and, somehow, she finds that she is the queen of light that brightens to its brim in the midst of darkness.

- EMPOWERMENT -

KNOWING YOUR KALI

Kali is the little rebellion voice in your heart; the one that time and again silently questions the norms, triggers a rage within and compels you to go on a journey of self-discovery. Kali is the powerful warrior energy that lives within every woman. She is the goddess of transformation and passion. Her form is powerful, enigmatic, mystic, passionate and healing. *Kali compels women to dig deep into their dark side and churn a new life out of the broken pieces.* The energy of Kali is often misunderstood as destructive. But it's on the fragments of negative elements that Kali guides us to build a new foundation of self-worth and dignity.

Kali evokes the confidence and power within us and banishes the feeling of helplessness. She lights the candle in the darkest, deepest core of our hearts to show us the light that we women crave and hunger for. She reminds us of the innate knowledge and wisdom that dwells within our heart, and gradually, with tough love and compassion, she trains us to become self-sufficient warriors, the protectors of our souls.

- EMPOWERMENT -

THE INNER WARRIOR

Kali awakens the inner warrior and directs the energy to create miracles beyond belief. She symbolises both spiritual and psychological liberation and is an archetype of a new awakening.

The warrior energy will initiate within you either after a long spell of suppression or when you are undergoing a spiritual awakening. When you embark on an inward spiritual journey, you are forced to look deeper into your flaws, your limitations, your past and your pain. Once you have learnt to embrace the darkness, you gradually move towards the light. Your warrior goddess will guide you to see your strengths, your energy and your essence.

She will work with you closely to prepare and train you to handle challenges gracefully. Her energy is transformative and you may feel extremely emotional or feisty while being trained, but once you have learnt to honour her energy, she will never let you down. Kali is beyond culture and race. She is the manifestation of the highest form of empowered energy.

- EMPOWERMENT -

WORDS TO EVOKE YOUR INNER WARRIOR

In this form or another, I am the empowered one. I sometimes manifest as Buddha, sometimes as a saint and sometimes I am the spark that triggers a change. I am the power, the healer. I am the fragrance that evokes passion and also the divine soothing smell of incense sticks. I am the one who evokes ego and I am the one who perishes pride.

I am Kali, the undefeatable warrior woman. I know the key to survival. I am not the one who gives up; I am not the one to retreat. I am the one who lights up the darkness. I am the one who fights the demons that destruct my inner harmony. I am the one who heals. I am the teacher, the seeker, the knower; my knowledge illuminates the world. I am the life in the stone that is worshipped. I am the essence of knowledge; I am wisdom.

I am the void that reflects the chaos and carves a new way of living. I am the intellect that guides philosophers to understand life from a higher perspective. I am the good in all goodness, the beauty in nature, the colour of flowers and the symmetry of a rainbow. *I am the truth in every lie, the authenticity in pretence.* I am the words of muteness, the imagination of blindness and the music of silence. I am the energy, the power, the pride. I am the light. I am Kali.

- EMPOWERMENT -

AGE OF KALI AND HER MESSAGE FOR WOMEN

Kali is asking all women to come together and take the world towards a higher level of humanity. When the masculine energy overpowers the natural balance of the universal totality, to recreate the balance, women must step up and take charge of bringing the world out of chaos. They must lead and show new ways of living with a humane intention that protects the soul from overindulging in materialistic manifestations. Women must set their own standard of beauty and love, on a vibration that respects their inner light. They must bring forth the spiritual dimension to this world that is living in an illusion of false reality.

History has witnessed numerous incidences when women have ignited their inner warrior to become change-makers. They intended to carve a better life for humanity, and every action had a higher purpose, devoid of selfishness and petty human limitations. Women have time and again reminded society that the sole purpose of human birth is to awaken to a new level of consciousness. Now, again, the time has come for women to join forces together and awaken their inner warrior collectively, as a tribe, to clear the chaos and upheaval. They must fight the demons of ignorance and bring a new level of quantum leap that will lead the human race to an age of wisdom and tolerance. The feminine energy must rise to give

- EMPOWERMENT -

spirit and soul to all the matter. She must plant kindness, faith, love, pride, dignity and wisdom to the lifeless manifestations born out of immature and aggressive masculine energy. The world must enter the age of Kali, of warrior women, and that is the only way it can survive through this current turbulence.

The age of Buddha and Kali is dawning. Women must raise their awareness to infuse wisdom and pride within it. They must send out vibrations of faith, courage and love. No matter where you are, and no matter what you do, you are Kali, and every time you tap into your inner consciousness, remember you are saving the world by joining forces with your pride of lionesses, silently and gradually leading the world towards light. Never think of yourself as insignificant. Your energy vibrates in the same dimension as those women who painted the history with their love and courage. All obstacles are an illusion of the mind. The soul, the inner fire, is free from social bondages and norms. All women have the power to make an inner transformation, irrespective of their circumstances. Nothing can banish and diminish the fire of wisdom and awakening that burns deep within your soul. Connect with your Kali and let her lead you to freedom and astuteness. No one else can do this for you; you alone must take

- EMPOWERMENT -

the first step towards a more dignified and awakened life. Remember, the forces of nature and abundance of universal energy breeds within a woman's soul. Spiritually, she is never really alone . A woman is constantly guided through dreams, books, songs, angels or just by instincts. The more she learns to listen to the voice that doesn't speak, the more effortlessly she will be able to open the closed chambers of ancient wisdom that lie guarded within her soul. She will gradually master the art of shedding the wounded skin that carries endless pain, unspoken words and diminished desires. With pride and grace, she will carefully decorate her soul with jewels of knowledge.

Once her inner knowledge is unveiled, she will connect deeply with fellow travellers and embrace the fact that she has been sent to sometimes heal and sometimes be healed in this journey that ultimately leads to liberation.

Believe in something you do not see.

Preparation

KNOWLEDGE

The beauty of a new world is emerging before my eyes,
A novel knowledge is diminishing the lies.
The more I indulge, the more I liberate,
Kali tells me this is a yogic state.
She constantly throbs my third eye,
Knocking the walls of deceit and sly,
Gradually, she tells me stories of past,
Kali, I surrender my life to your task.

−Ekta

–Ekta

- KNOWLEDGE -

THE SPIRIT OF LOTUS

Women in any unpleasant situation or crisis should take inspiration from the lotus flower. It is a manifestation of a woman's energy and a perfect metaphor of her life. Just as the lotus, immersed in mud, rises every day to a new life and reflects awakened wisdom, so does a woman in crisis have to learn to remain unharmed by the negative mess that is pulling her down and learn to awaken her inner wisdom. She has to detach herself from the distressing chaos and find a place within her heart which connects her to her higher intuitive self. She will find her empowered energy within her enlightened liberated heart.

Our inner warrior woman reminds us constantly to clear our minds of all negative thoughts. It's natural to feel low sometimes and build up a few spots of black energy within, but to succumb to darkness and base our life upon it, is ignorance. Women must constantly and consciously reprogramme their minds to restructure the pattern of their thoughts. Just as nature constantly washes off the dust with rain and revives this human abode, similarly, let the white divine light shower your soul and free you of negative binds. A woman's soul is not meant to nurture evil; its essence is to sprout life. Release yourself constantly from the chains that block your mind and let your Kali guide you to become the wild, fearless and loving lotus of life.

- KNOWLEDGE -

CLEANSING THE SOUL

Kali herself embodies women time and again and reminds them to liberate their innocent heart from any soul harming thoughts.

Every thought of harm will manifest with intensity and prosper under the protection of a woman's creative energy. A thought doesn't have any essence. Our choices give it power and direction. Femininity is the energy of creation and preservation. What a woman holds with caution in her heart flourishes with abundance; both pain and pleasure. Kali thus warns women to be aware of their deepest desires, their fleeting wishes, their prayers and their fury. Each has the power to manifest and take the shape of a woman's heart. The power that infuses love can also wage a war. Every woman must learn to harness this power and give it a direction of love and compassion. Her passion must be devoid of her pain. Every moment is a chance for you to preserve with love what you create with love and also to perish with compassion what does not need protection.

Release yourself constantly from the chains that block your mind and let your Kali guide you to become the wild, fearless and loving light of life.

- KNOWLEDGE -

LIVING WITHOUR FEAR

What is living without fear? Why does it take a lifetime for women to realise that fear was a mere illusion? When a soul insults its energy by living the illusion of fear, then to trigger a momentum of change, the force of Kali brings forth the circumstances that make the illusion real. This is done to test your faith, your passion and ultimately to raise your wisdom to the reality that fear is the reflection of your doubt. Your inner warrior is defeated by no one but your own doubt that manifests fear. The battle is lost when you contemplate your loss and brood on unrealistic reality. Honour your warrior. Let it rise to its potential; let her raise your inner flame; let her burn fear by fighting the worst. Once you overcome the illusion and rise above your fear, your energy will guide you to truth. There is no wall, no obstacle, no tears, no sorrow, no pain, no struggle; it's all an illusion and a sign of your diminished energy.

Every woman must constantly remind herself that nothing is more harmful than the thought of an impending harm. *The enemy lies within and so does your warrior.* You have the tools to empower the enemy of fear and doubt or to harness your warrior. Kali silently gives you the choice. She secretly guides you towards a fearless, complete life of truth and liberation, but the choice remains with you. You will manifest what you follow.

Be aware of what you are not. Rest is what you are.

Acceptance

TRUTH

Kali speaks in silence,
Enveloping the void of the dark.
I see light, shapes and symbols,
Words linger a soul stirring spark.
The spirals of the world dance in ecstasy,
Portals of an unknown dimension,
Break illusion of childlike fantasy.
I speak to a voice, that sings the song of my soul.
In my dreams, I am alive, my soul is whole.
The truth is alive, the hidden also appears,
Like a mirror, it reflects my joy, my fears.
I am Kali, the origin of truth and real,
I am the dream, the seen and the seer.

–Ekta

- TRUTH -

DREAMS ARE MESSAGES FROM ANOTHER DIMENSION

The cyclic pattern of day and night is nature's honour and delight. When the world sleeps at night, that's the time when the warrior woman rests her guard and opens the portals of her energy to embrace an alternate vibration that turns lucid in the darkness of the night.

Kali guides her gently, as the awakened woman's soul travels to heal and design the patterns of codes that enable her free soul to fly in psychedelic ecstasy.

A woman's soul is extremely sensitive, enabling her to feel the shift in every vibration around her. This becomes prominent in the depth of the night. Your dreams are not a reflection of your thoughts; they are the codes of your liberation. Your dreams are messages from another dimension. Every song, pattern, colour and symbol is a code to decipher the reality of events that you witness in your waking state. Oblivious of the outer drama, this is a time when you can travel through dimensions and understand the putative nature of your intuitions.

The truth is that for the awakened woman, sleep is the wakened state; a time when her soul defies the law of time and space and in a glorified state silently tames the inner fire so she may follow the unique mandalic patterns of her life.

The intricate patterns of a mandala are akin to a woman's soul. Every symbol and colour of a mandala is placed perfectly to complete a symmetric design that reflects our current spiritual journey. There can be no judgement of the design, as it is the spiritual truth in its most authentic self and is unique to the one who connects to its patterns. A complete mandala is a blueprint of one's past, present and future. When viewed in totality, the delicateness of its design can become daunting, leading to denial of its understanding.

When an empowered woman rises above the ashes like a phoenix and looks at the totality of her perfectly symmetric and beautifully designed mandala of life, the initial reaction is one of denial. 'Am I worth it?' she questions. 'Is this my beauty?' she wonders.

Deluded by the words of the world that she knows less than everyone else, she reaches out for help and shares her dilemma with fellow travellers. Some mock at her imaginations, others sympathise, some empathise, and a large section of them fear what will happen if this woman realises that this in fact is her reality. It is at this point when women must rely on no one but their highest enlightened self and seek out guidance through dreams.

- TRUTH -

To understand her true power, she must view every curve, every pattern with a fearless heart and divine intention.

Every intricate, complicated pattern must be felt and interpreted with utmost simplicity. The more one calms the tempestuous mind, the more lucid and vivid the patterns become. Kali reminds every human soul that their outer self is a cover, a role that they play in the complicated patterns of life.

When one connects to the simple fact that truth is the energy that we are and the vibrations that we emit, then every complex problem reveals its simple solution.

- TRUTH -

DISCOVERING YOUR TRUTH

Who am I? What is my energy? What is my past? What is my future? These are the common questions of every inquisitive mind.

The 'I' in you is an illusion, a fake layer that is created by our human consciousness to cope with the laws of the physical plane. An illusion that is perceived in variety by varied minds. Then, who is this real you? To find your essence, your own fragrance, your energy, you must first conquer this 'I'. Let the illusion diminish gradually and let the outer noises fade in the vicinity of the only voice that matters – the voice of your soul: the voice of Kali. To listen to her words, you must first learn to disable your ears. To behold her vision, you must master the art of seeing without eyes. To feel her energy, you must fade the physical boundaries of your human body. *Your Kali lies deep within where only thought can hear, mind can see and soul can feel.* She will tell you all about you, but like a plain canvas, you must first be ready to be painted in her colours. She will show you who you are but only after you cross the fire of vanity. And after you have merged your 'I' into her fire, you will find that in reality she will only magnify it for the world to see. She will fan your flame and induce it with her own dynamic force to make your power invincible, and suddenly there will be no need to know the 'I'. You will be Kali and she will be you – your warrior energy.

- TRUTH -

FOLLOW YOUR CALLING

What calls you from the deepest forest? What is the sound that sparkles a light within you? What is the colour that seems to be in synchronisation with some deep thought within you? What are the words that time and again seem to be ringing in your ears, trying to open a crevice in your soul? What is the symbol, the pattern that resonates with your journey and path of your life? Every woman must be more mindful of these subtle indications that are knocks to her profound powers. Every woman must be aware of the sounds, the smells, the visions that cross her path. Her inner Kali will time and again remind her that there are no coincidences. Everything has been planned for her to realise the full potential of her wildness, her warrior soul.

Intuitions are the energies that constantly play with your aura, your soul, in an attempt to make you aware of the truth of oneness. Kali is you and you are Kali. She dwells in your folly and your victory. She is your tears; she is your smile. She is your anger; she is your virtue. Let her guide you to show the impeccable mirror of truth. Let her be your voice. Let her evoke the great intuitive power bestowed to women. Let her harness your skills of soul and wash away the toxins collected over lifetimes. Let doubt mitigate gradually, for where faith lives, Kali lives.

You are both: the seeker and what you seek.

Realisation

AWAKENING

Kali is quiet,
She is resting her bones,
She has fought with vigour,
Opened my eyes to truth unknown.
Rest Kali, you have done your task,
Awakened my warrior, what more could I ask?
I resisted, I denied, I didn't want to face my fear,
But like a mother, like a guide you embraced my tears.
Graceful Kali, you are the rightful might,
You brought me to the steps of counter divine,
Sleep Kali, let my warrior nurture the inner light,
Wisdom of Buddha is guiding my ignorance and clearing the sight.

–Ekta

- AWAKENING -

THE AWAKENED WOMAN

Embracing your dark side is not an easy task. Some people shy away from it or deny its existence; when in reality no energy can manifest in singularity.

Every living, vibrating energy has a dark side, a focal point of cumulative energy which dwells in darkness. If given the right direction and controlled wisely, this dark energy becomes the catalyst of a life-changing moment for a person. Don't ignore the existence of anger, greed, jealousy, hate or vagueness within you. Embrace it, accept it and take charge of its direction. Tear asunder from the place of denial to the comforts of acceptance. From darkness will rise the brightest fire within you that will set forth a new light in your life.

Our inner warrior woman constantly reminds us to find our unique light in the depth of our own darkness, to face our shortcomings with grace and turn them into positive manifestations with love and patience. Hate has no place in a heart that yearns to be free.

Kali: the warrior, the enchanted awakened light within every woman, the healer, the mystic, the wild one, the love that dwells in the energy of a woman, is asking constantly to remember the importance of letting go of hatred.

- AWAKENING -

Many awakened women, because of their ability to comprehend and feel more intently, are able to realise the truth of every fake relation around them. This can lead to disappointment and sometimes hatred towards a particular energy. She is furious at having been taken for granted. She is angry over being let down time and again by the ones she has trusted. Now that her Kali has awakened, she recognises her powers and demands her rightful place in society and in her relationships. It's the light within her that makes the darkness in others more lucid.

Any woman who is going through a phase of such inner awakening must be reminded that it is also important to keep forgiving the ignorant as she elevates in her knowledge. The more a woman liberates from hatred, the stronger she can open her heart to feel and nurture her intuitive and spiritual light. A woman must learn to forgive those energies that have not yet got the insight to honour her strength. She must constantly heal her wounds and simultaneously send healing vibrations to her perpetrator. This is the only way to be liberated from the invisible ties that have connected her to the energy she has been tangled with from many births. She must learn to love and heal to bring an end to a cycle that accelerates with hatred and liberates with love. Don't let hate close the doors of opportunity and insight. Don't let guilt and pain entrap you so much that you hinder your own inner growth.

Trust your Kali as she holds your hand and leads you towards your highest liberated self. Let her show you your true powers and help you heal the wounds of lifetimes. Let her sparkle the light within you and open your heart, your inner lotus, with love and only love.

Let your warrior woman awaken you silently while the world sleeps in ignorance.

- AWAKENING -

THE CANDLE OF CURIOSITY

A burning desire in every wild warrior woman's heart is to know and understand the truth of her existence. Time and again, you may have found your energy drifting towards a place of curiosity, a yearning to know the unknown. This inward journey is the reality of your existence. Our energy dances in conjoined halves of masculine and feminine. The masculine arouses the questions but they are inert and un-animated till the feminine infuses it with passion and light.

Your inner warrior is reminding you that every question that arises in your heart is a chance to go deep into your own depths, layer by layer. *The answers that lie within the swirls of the questions are waiting to be unveiled by illuminated knowledge.* The ignorance of not knowing is merely an illusion. In reality, every answer lies within our core. Women know this and it's this mere belief that enables them to harness adaptability with ease. Her intuition becomes her guiding light as she embarks on an unknown journey or undertakes a new challenge. This is the reason why any new role is easily embraced by women. She breezes with ease from a lone traveller to burning in passion with her lover. She embraces the sprout of a new life with grace, and with compassion nurtures novel dreams within her heart and into the soul of her offspring.

- AWAKENING -

Acceptance comes naturally to the female dimension too, thus giving her the insight to embrace the time to let go for the saplings to spread far and let the forest grow.

While the world amazes at the source of this impeccable talent, a woman's heart preserves every new knowledge with utmost care, for she knows that it's within her hands that the universe has laid the responsibility to manifold her learning and keep the fire of curiosity and learning alighted.

Curiosity is merely a play of Kali's energy that is abundantly generating within a passionate heart. Your inner warrior is constantly guiding you to combat ignorance by giving fire to every question and yearning to learn more. With every answer, clouds of illusion will be torn asunder and the fire of knowing will be alighted with love.

- AWAKENING -

BEFRIENDING THE DARKNESS

Many women who are living on their own, circumstantially or by choice, are constantly also living with the fear of loneliness. These are strong women who have had the power to voice opinions and challenge norms, and yet loneliness compels them to succumb to self-harm or depression. Gradually they forget and neglect their inner power, their Kali, and become influenced by the powers that lie outside them. This fear of being on their own while living in a society clearly validates that society offers no respite to the need of security.

Every woman must learn that she is never really alone, that she has the power to raise her vibrations and attract the right people into her life, that she can use her time and resources to benefit the less fortunate and make the world her family. The fear of loneliness almost every time leads the woman to an energy where she attracts only weak, fearful people in her life, which further leads to another cycle of hurt and deceit. Strength of mind is not just a game of action; it is also a power of silence and calm.

The warrior Kali will only bloom into a full thousand petal lotus if she has learnt to calm her randomness, her wild side, her Buddha. Kali is the true energy, the power, the inner strength, the perfect dance, the melodious voice, the talent,

- AWAKENING -

the life, the laughter, the pride and the truth within each woman. Honour this truth and let no fear overshadow the rightful divine darkness that illuminates your life. Do not let fear of loneliness overpower your intellect, for you are never really alone. Do not fear deceit, for none but you are your own true companion, and never let ignorance dwindle the light of knowledge within you.

Within her, a woman will find the absolute wholeness; within her she will find the eternal happiness, and within her, she will find the true love. Our inner warrior keeps reminding us to constantly raise our energy by focussing on inner Buddha, and that is the only way to find the true society of loving and trustful people in our lives. The only way to find the tribe that reflects our vibrations.

Decorate your soul; the body will instantly illuminate.

Nurture

WISDOM

The veil has fallen,
The truth is revealed.
Vague dreams and visions
Are reality of a birth I had lived.
In awe I relish this blissful boon,
Opening the gates of a distant moon.
My path is yours; it had always been.
Our chord is connected by a timeless stream.
In your guidance I see it lucidly now.
Kali, I surrender with love, with heartfelt gratitude to your power, today I bow.

−Ekta

–Ekta

- WISDOM -

KALI AND BUDDHA

Kali and Buddha are polarities of spiritual wisdom. One works towards light, while the other dances in darkness. One nurtures wisdom, while the other breeds randomness, but both lead to a supreme spiritual ecstasy that is parallel to no other joy. Women will find that at times they are guided to feed the calm within them, and sometimes they will crave for their wild spontaneity. It's vital to note that both polarities compliment and complete each other.

A woman who has initiated her inner warrior and taken a stand in life will pass through many tests and struggles. She will be ridiculed, judged and mocked. When this happens, she must call out for help to her spiritual polarity – her Buddha. Her inner wisdom will gently guide the wildness to flow freely without fear, and dance randomly to its own music. This is the importance of evoking your inner Buddha while calling out for your warrior archetype. Your inner Buddha will help the warrior within you to channelise the energy in the right direction. A clear example of this can be seen in our current society.

When a woman fights years of abuse and initiates her Kali, she gradually finds strength to stand for herself and take some strong steps that lead her to her rightful place in life.

- WISDOM -

She may decide to punish the abuser or sometimes leave an abusive marriage and move on in life on her own. Her Kali guides her to fight the inner war and win it, but once it's done, then comes the tougher battle. Her morals and her belief will be challenged every day. She will be forced to doubt her decisions. If she delays initiating her inner Buddha to guide and reassure her, she may become a victim of depression. This is the reason why some strong women fall into the traps of manipulative energies again and again. They have learnt to initiate the inner battle but haven't learnt to cease it with calm. Just as the fire that is evoked in a prayer must be left to cool down, so must a woman who has initiated her inner fire then cool down with wisdom and logical reasoning of her actions. She will gradually understand that her energy does not need outer validation.

We all have felt the pain and sufferings. We all have met our challenges and lived them on their face. It's vital to remember that each one of us has a part within that remains broken, shattered, twisted and scarred; an uncared for, abandoned and lonely part. This part was screaming and shouting for attention, but oblivious to its plead, all we cared was to see our tears. We know it exists, yet we choose to live in denial. Our ignorance gradually became our stubbornness.

- WISDOM -

This part has been constantly reminding us of the gains that we achieved each day, the joy that shaped us, the failures that taught us, the simple smiles that existed around us, but unfortunately it was ignored. It's never too late to awaken to truth. Listen to that tiny part, nourish it with love, think its thoughts, and one day, gradually, that part will merge into your wholeness.

Within this wholeness, a woman will discover the seed of her spiritual existence and move on towards her higher self.

- WISDOM -

THE VOID OF WISDOM

Void is an uncomfortable state. Often because, in our human incarnation, we are mostly conscious of our current state, where we are alive and things are animated around us. Our mind wanders in the past or the future but the anchor point remains in the present moment. We travel to past memories or future dreams, inspired by a present life situation.

It's vital to remember that neither the beginning is in our memory, nor is the end known. This makes the life that we have around us the most known state and our comfort zone. Often, especially during happy moments, we are deluded in believing that this will be an endless state of existence for us. The moment our soul feels an urge to move away from this state and enter the realms of our origin, or understand the timeless end, we enter a state of transformation. This is the moment, when, soul desires to leave the comfort zone and recognise its true nature. This is when the soul vibrates in the void or nothingness alone. Everything is quiet and numb. To understand the journey, time and again, enter the depth within.

It's ok to feel detached sometimes to cleanse your aura, as long as you remember to come back with the lessons you have understood and shine brighter. Don't be afraid to enter

- WISDOM -

self-introspection. Your inner warrior initiates it at the time when you are ready to recognise its power. That is when the seed of knowing will be sprouted. Each one of us will time and again have an urge to detach from the world and understand the sound of silence that vibrates within. This is not just a powerful spiritual ritual; it's also a very divine cleansing process. This void is the place where emotions are mostly pragmatic; mind is open for a new perspective and soul is ready to let go of what weighs it down. Be comfortable with the thought of leaving your illusion of a comfort zone, a temporary state of your being. Your true self knows the void. Enter it fearlessly to unearth the knowledge and wisdom that is meant for your journey.

Float aimlessly for a while, step out of the drama to become the witness sometimes. Do not judge what you feel. Just be, and trust that this nothingness is also your known state of being. Embrace the void because that is the place from where your life will truly begin.

- WISDOM -

BREAKING THE SPIRAL

Kali is reminding women the importance of constantly shedding past pain in order to grow internally. We women become victims of our own bondages and thoughts. As we awaken to some new truths, the reality of certain relationships around us shake our strong belief in love and sincerity. We are sometimes unable to understand the shallow thoughts of certain minds. Our past perceptions are broken and this sudden awakening can at times hinder or temporarily, cease one's spiritual progress.

This is also the time when women become victims of isolation and depression. While the world is persuading her to see the good in everything, her inner wisdom is fighting a battle between the fake and the real. She is waking to a new truth, adding new colours and changing the whole picture of life in her mind. As her intuition increases, so does the dilemma and burden of knowing the truth of her existence. She cries over times she has humiliated her own soul.

This is the time when a woman must tap into her healing energy of Kali and learn to let go of the burden of guilt and pain. Through the depth of darkness, she must let Kali guide her to find a light of hope.

Kali is reminding her that the actions of others should not be a cause of worry and distress to her, as it is not her responsibility to either punish or blame. The occurrence of every event is, in reality, a healing process. Her only purpose is to heal the wounds that have opened on this first step of awakening. She must not stop on this journey of awakening, threatened and deluded by false illusions. Instead, she must forgive her soul and others as she moves on towards her eternal spiritual journey. Kali will give her the strength to embrace the truth and set her free from the painful spiral so she may move ahead with a more peaceful heart.

The void is the place from where life begins.

Healing

LOVE

Kali what is this game?
What people value is just a name.
They admire the beauty that can be seen.
Say vague words that have no gleam.
What about the treasure that lives beneath the skin?
What about the filth that grows within?
Kali says it's all my play,
It's your own light that has to lead their way,
Let not their flaws kill your joy,
You all are nothing but my toy.
Let me remind you of your deed,
You reap at the end what you seed.

—Ekta

- LOVE -

MELODY OF A SOUL

Soul is nothing but a fragment of the energy torn asunder out of nothingness. The energy reverberates eternally the vibrations that were attributed to it in its origin.

When the energy enters the body, it transfers the vibrations to a form that can be easily comprehended by our five senses, but only once they are awakened to a spiritual state. Our soul constantly sends us indications of its infinite truth. If you feel drawn to a particular piece of music, feel a strange warmth, smell a sudden divine scent or experience coincidence or visions that defy time and space, you may in reality be getting closer towards knowing the seed of your existence and your vibrational melody or the melody of your soul. The more you self-observe, the more you sharpen the senses that exist beyond the five senses. You will see the colours that have no describable vocabulary and gradually understand why a soul is attracted towards liberation so ardently. An empowered, awakened woman's inner warrior can hear what we cannot, see what was beyond description and perceive what we cannot possibly possibility dream of. She can connect to the vibrational melody of her soul and see the origin, experience the nothingness and understand the fact that there is no beginning and no end. All our existence is nothing but a journey towards understanding the origin and recognising the melody of our all-knowing, all-encompassing soul.

- LOVE -

MERGING IN ABSOLUTE LOVE

There is no denying that women understand and experience love with much more intensity than any other vibrating energy. The feminine energy is the origin and the culmination of love. But for every woman to preserve the balance of love, it's vital to fearlessly tread towards the authenticity of its existence.

Perishable love has its own limit. That limit lies in its mortality and its capability. The seed of this love sprouts from your heart which has a limited capability to express and understand emotions. This journey will bring you to a place of loneliness, dejection and darkness until you learn to generate more energy and preserve the already existing love. But like all journeys, it has an end. Bound by our mortality, this journey ends on the physical plane. This perishable love is like a sweet filler in our timeless journey. It can also be compared to a fresh fragrance. As long as the source is around, the beauty of its existence remains. Your emotions toggle in response to the experience around you. Only after you follow the path of perishable love, may you embark on a more rigorous journey of absolute love. Absolute love starts from the point from where the perishable love stabilises. The point where the sweetness of love morphs into a habit, a oneness and a natural extension of self. Most people will find themselves satiated with the flavours of perishable love and that's fine. It will lead to a good life with possibly more good times than harsh moments. But if you wish to experience love with a boundless capability, then you have to tread the path of absolute love. So, what is absolute love? It's love whose origin is seeded in the eternal nothingness and whose end is in nothingness too.

When you love someone with a view devoid of 'I' love and 'Mine', the motive redefines itself instantly. Absolute love aims for more and demands more too. Its journey expands from just being a lover, friend or a teacher; it requires each to be the other's healer. It requires the ability to see beyond the frames of flesh and bone and understand the energy that resides within each other. It requires going to the depth of nothingness to decipher the truth behind choosing each other as travellers in this time frame. What did you both want to learn? What spiritual lesson lies in this union? What needs to be healed with love?

Absolute love is a journey of spiritually liberating each other as we walk. There is grace in every step, patience and gratitude in every action and surrender at every breath. The soul that chose to spend time and space with you chose to go through this journey to help you learn some lessons. Every act performed to deliver the lesson is divine. Every emotion, of anger, dejection, love or hate, is a divine plan. When you start looking at a relationship with that divinity, expectations of getting loved back shift to gratitude of being loved. There is an unbreakable trust, an understanding. Absolute love not only brings love in one heart, it expands that love to every force of the universe. There is no end and no beginning of this love: the eternal absolute love.

When you experience a union of absolute love, love illuminates the darkest corners of your mind. The thin veil between the divine and lover merges and love itself becomes a devotion to the supreme.

So, what lies beyond love and what lies before love is just love, because all that there is, is just pure, absolute love.

EXPANDING THE GRACE

Everything that happens in life happens because of a reason. The energy of every small to big, grateful and ungrateful event is triggered because of a force that has been inspired by a conjoined universal energy that encompasses your energy as well. Our ego tries to find the reason on root level; a reason derived from what it feels and perceives from a human perspective that is coated with sometimes insignificant facts and pain. This brings forth hurt, anger and self-abuse. The reason may look valid and reasonable and may serve you as a guide to make choices but Kali is reminding you that the choices made from this energy will entrap and force you to go through the same event again and again until you learn to find a reason derived from wisdom. *Wisdom and love gives the situation a completely different perspective.* It may seem a weak escape to many whose aggression serves their ego, but for those who are hungry to nourish their soul this is the nectar that sinks to the barren patches and heals the wound forever.

The inner warrior is telling women that not every battle has to be won; some battles are lost in this dimension but won on an empowered level, that completely liberates you from the pain of suffering. Kali is asking all women to choose their battles with love, wisdom and faith; knowing that their Kali thirsts for unadulterated love, not pride.

What speaks to you in silence, stays with you in chaos.

Reflecting

PATIENCE

Listen to silence, it has a sound,
Embrace its echo, submerge deeper till you are found,
Kali resides within your darkest zone,
Awaken her with love, she is your own.
You did what you could, you made your plans,
Now surrender abundantly and dance in her trance.
Find your power, your reason to be,
Kali, let me be you; you become me.

–Ekta

- PATIENCE -

THE SUBTLE CHANGES

Change is inevitable. It is not something that happens in just one moment in life. It's something that we experience every moment of our life. Every breath is a moment of change, of our thoughts and energy level. A woman feels this change with a much stronger power than anyone else because her energy is not just embracing this change constantly but also questioning it. She is blessed with the innate ability to move to a new dimension every moment and simultaneously comprehend each realm with compassion and wisdom. On a physical plane, this energy is much more subtle, displayed by the inherent ability of a woman to multitask and manage varied roles with grace and love. This is not something that women need to glorify or be bashful about; it's something that a woman must naturally embrace as a grace.

A woman has a natural connection with nature. She understands the songs of the birds, the symmetry of patterns and the need to follow a system. She also understands the fire that is constantly raving, raging and churning under the crust of the earth. She understands the life that is continuously thriving and moving under the calm sea. This, a woman understands because she is an extension of nature itself. Like a tree, she stands firm on the nurturing ground. Like a river, she flows with excitement towards a new beginning, a new skill. Like wind, she envelops the heart of every task she undertakes, and like fire, she initiates passion and becomes the catalyst of changes.

A woman who has sensed the power of Kali within her will know that within the realms of the known, lies a magical instrument that is waiting to be explored. Digging deep into something that will soothe her soul; a woman sees herself as more than just a body. She yearns to find the root of the fragrance that stirs her soul, a song that her spirit has been longing for, a smell that matches the vibrations of her fragrance, a voice that sings the hymns she has secretly heard. Its music is unique for every woman and naturally tunes in sync with the woman it's made for.

Every woman owns her own secret musical instrument, song, poem or fragrance. Something that elevates and dances to her thoughts. Once she learns to hear its music, she learns to understand and embrace change. She learns to conquer fear, tame her wildness and nurture her wise self: her Kali. Such a woman is wise enough to understand that change is the life that runs in her veins, her thoughts, her courage and her pride.

- PATIENCE -

POTENT POWER OF SILENCE

Kali wants women to rave this potent power of silence that their deepest selves possess. Unlike the common belief that opinions must be voiced instantly, your inner warrior woman is asking you to pause, to think, to reflect and to indulge in an inner dialogue before opening the gates of your mouth outwardly. It is essential to speak up for one's self-respect, but it is far more essential to first heal the inner wounds and reflect on the situations in silence and solitude. This ignites the flames of wisdom and strengthens the power of spoken words. When your inner Kali awakens, she brings with her a storm of past memories. Hidden secrets are unearthed, soul is scraped to its deepest core and a plethora of emotions arise from the dead. Kali warns that though this darkness is essential to reach the flame of inner light, what's even more vital is to indulge in this journey with an outward silence and an inner dialogue. To hear the sound of your soul, to discover the uniqueness of your essence and finally to meditate upon the power of nothingness. *When thoughts come to a point of nothing, from there then arises a new light that enlightens the aura with wisdom and grace.* Before a woman wages a war with the world, she must first win the inner battle. For this, she has to quieten the outward noises and find her voice of Kali. Only then, her spoken words will have the strength to conquer the demons that she has challenged.

- PATIENCE -

FEMININE GRACE

Kali, the dark goddess of light, the enigmatic persona of inner strength, the magnificent spirit of life, is urging women to remember that fighting for the right does not imply that the woman should lose her innate feminine grace. The grace of soul should stay firm just like a rock that stands proudly in the midst of a turbulent waterfall or river. The rock eventually becomes an anchor to those who need to be saved.

In true terms, pain purifies a woman's soul and inspires her to tap into the inner beauty, her dormant Kali. She perceives a new truth and experiences events as a new spectator after her Kali has awoken. Her new truth, her Kali, demands justice for her pain but with patience and grace.

Like a hunting tigress, her inner Kali awaits the right moment and gradually, in the meantime, she strips the unwanted and allows the light to heal. Kali reminds women that pain is inevitable sometimes but our reaction to pain is only justified and true once we have learnt to rest and heal. She must embrace the pain, the deceit, the humiliation with open arms and then gradually prepare to attack only after she has been healed on soul level. This will give her fight for justice power and grace. Any attack that is planted out of pain will result in deeper pain and revenge.

- PATIENCE -

An enlightened wild woman does not seek revenge; she seeks an understanding of her pain. She seeks the wisdom of truth in her perpetrator and she seeks learning. She seeks healing. She seeks grace. She seeks Kali and she seeks to become the voice of Kali. She will speak the truth with conviction and she seeks to be heard. She will dance the dance of justice without pride and revenge. She seeks liberation from a cycle of pain for both her and the un-awakened one. She seeks the strength to fight with grace but only after allowing her inner Buddha and Kali to come into balance.

Kali smiles as she repeatedly reminds women that their inner warrior woman will only dance with grace if the war that evokes her movements is the war of truth.

Change can only be understood by being constant.

Recieving

GRACE

Kali whispers in my ear,
I am not around, I am within here,
Fiercely she dances to the rhythms that heal,
Kali, let me join the ecstatic zeal.
Hold nothing that slows your steps she says,
My tribe is not for faint hearted displays.
Liberate your demons to join my pace,
Kali, oh what a glorious face!

–Ekta

—Ekta

- GRACE -

BEAUTY OF A WOMAN

What is the beauty of a woman? What makes a woman beautiful? Her resilience, her inner strength, her wolf-like protective nature towards her offspring, her randomness, her childlike curiosity over matters which her soul has mastered eternally, her grace, her poise in the most chaotic times, her humbleness, her willingness to share wisdom and love, her fire, her inner warrior.

Not that women have no right to beautify their body, but just as Kali radiates her femininity with pride of being who she is, every woman must also attain a respect for the vessel her soul has chosen. Do not judge your outer self and persona by the way the ignorant perceive it. Kali, the fierce one, walks with the rhythm of life, oblivious to who is watching her random dance. She celebrates her divine existence abundantly, and with her radiating darkness she fights the fearful demons of negativity that the most valiant ones evade. Her beauty is her confidence; her beauty is her love; her beauty is her unmatched vigour and radiance.

Kali is constantly teaching every woman to find within her the timeless beauty of intuitive inner strength that needs no outward validation.

- GRACE -

THE MANDALA OF LIFE

Kali reminds us that we are nothing but energy portals and travellers in this bodily frame. This body which is a vehicle to move from one birth to another in order to live, observe and just be. Kali warns women that over obsession of this frame is just like being an ignorant gardener who decorates the walls that surround his flowers and ignores the essence of his flowers. He will eventually be surrounded by admirers of the wall, not the flowers. *An empowered woman honours the beauty and fragrance of her soul and of those that she chooses to surround herself with.* She guards the realm of her soul fiercely from the unwanted energy and consciously refuses to follow the light of ignorance. She knows that the light that shines from within is her true beauty and strength.

She honours the cycle of nature and blossoms in every season of her life. For her, ageing is the opportunity to collect stories and share them with her fellow travellers. It's the time to heal and be healed. It's her opportunity to thrill in meeting the souls that have passed her in many lifetimes in numerous forms. It's her chance to learn and rejoice in the journey of lifetimes. Kali relishes the energy of a woman who ages not just physically but, in her wisdom, her grace and her essence as well.

- GRACE -

UNDERSTANDING TRUST

Women are innately prone to trust more. Once they commit to a relationship, they give without inhibitions and connect on the deepest emotional level. Their love is pure; their care is selfless and their courage is powerful. A woman in love can face the deepest and biggest turmoils of life with grace and beauty. All she needs is the reflection of her love in the eyes of her lover. She knows that something is missing but she trusts that her love will clear the doubts away. A woman in love is like the purest form of fire that lightens up dark times and absorbs all that is thrown within. The highest manifestation of power and life. To all such women, I bow and hope that no one ever breaks the trust of such true love. But if it has been done to you, then do not fret tears of helplessness. Don't ever feel like a fool for trusting with all your heart. Never regret being so preposterous that you could not see the truth. The truth is that you are power, glory, faith and creation.

You are the life force in all lifeless manifestations. You are the healer, the teacher, the lover and the destroyer. You have the purest heart that knows how to love and you also have the fiercest strength that understands how to survive. You walk, unashamed of making wrong choices because they were the calling of your heart and you have shown time and again that you possess the strength to walk with pride on the decisions that you make. You are free. You are Kali.

Experience the understanding.

Knowing

SURRENDER

The phantom of arrogance,
Closes many gates of knowing.
The ego deceives you in deception,
Questions your humble act of bowing?
Kali warns, do not be misled,
When power is released,
The constraints of bondage flee.
Like a bird you fly in an open space,
Surrender with love, receive the grace.

–Ekta

- SURRENDER -

POLARITIES OF LIFE

The polarities of life make the incomplete energy whole. It is in totality that we find our balance. It's in shadow that we find the light; when inner consciousness merges with the outer consciousness, truth with deceit, divine with evil, past with future, dark with light, ego with soul, vice with virtue, man with woman and chaos with order. It's within the polarities that a woman must strive to find her true nature, her own unique fragrance. It's very natural for a woman to lose her soul in the midst of extremities and get to a point when directions seem to fade. When her honour, pride, dignity and her essence are being challenged, leading her to doubt her light, her divinity, her virtue and her power. She believes the demonic opposites to be her true nature and is dragged into darkness, vice and chaos. It's at this point when she must call on her Kali and bring the balance back in her life. She must fight and go beyond what can be seen, to look deeper for her soul that is beyond life and death, beyond judgements and rewards. She must find order within the chaos by embracing the polarities as the law of nature; the nature that itself is governed by the Kali within her. It may mean restructuring and reviving the old beliefs, but if a woman at that point, keeping faith within her innate power, moves ahead with surrender, she will unleash powers to turn her pain into a cause that raises the human consciousness to a new level of goodness.

- SURRENDER -

SPIRITUAL DANCERS OF THE SAME TRIBE

The illusion of detachment is perhaps the most pristine work of the universe. Each one of us is a result of the mass deception created by the ignorant innocence of the human mind. 'What is mind?' Kali asks. 'A collection of thoughts superimposed by imprints of experiences? When a mere thought is not stable, how can the world manifested out of this womb be assured of being an authentic representation of the truth?'

Every human being has a unique lens to view and comprehend the idea of life. *The female dimension within us has an advantage here. She has been bestowed with the ability to refine and adjust her perception by moving rapidly between dimensions.* Every moment, she creates a novel thought, nurtures it and destroys an old perception, based on what her soul has experienced in its silent travels.

Your inner warrior is constantly distorting your view of life and presenting you with that what's real. When she performs that ritual, you may feel the pain of excursion of old beliefs, you may find that the outer voices are nothing but a distraction and you may realise that you have the power to harness the capability to shed this layer of illusion and see the reality of our existence. Connections of blood are a role play for us to learn our lessons; in reality it's the energy that binds us

- SURRENDER -

all together. Kali will show you the mirror that will reflect your aura in every being. Your soul extends from your vibration and spreads to every flower, tree, human, animal and being around you. 'But, is that possible?' You will ask with fear. Your inner warrior will give you a gentle push and with vigour she will raise the curtains of the phantom vision to display the actual scene. 'But it was a play,' she will say with compassion in her eyes. 'Your only task was to observe and prepare yourself for your dimensional travels.'

Every spark of energy is a manifestation of the mind; in reality we all are just one huge ball of fire which has the power to collectively rise to a new level of awakening so we may together leap to the next dimension and learn new lessons. Kali warns that the key word here is 'together'. Your tiniest amount of inner work has the ability to create the powerful ripple of awakening so those who have lost their path may remember their true nature. This sense of detachment and connectedness is bizarre and baffling, yet at the same time , it's empowering too.

Kali is reminding every warrior woman that she has the innate ability to focus on her inner world, be unaffected by the outer world and yet have a sense of connectedness.

To know and understand that each of us, irrespective of our gender and culture, is just human is the knowledge of the wise one, but to know that we are nothing but a spark of the same energy, is the knowledge of the seer.

Kali reminds us that women create their world with an experience based on their soul's imprints, not mind. Her heart leads; her mind follows. She is a natural seer, and this is her potent power.

- SURRENDER -

A NOVEL VIEW OF SELF

What are self-esteem and self-worth? They are nothing but honouring your warrior woman. It's appalling to see women trying to find their worth in all eyes except theirs. Your soul is waiting for your call, your awakening, and that light only sparks from within. The moment you try to find the sparkle of your colour outside, you only reflect the opinions and views that are adulterated by negative vibes.

To find your aura soul colour, your innate fragrance, your Kali, is your purpose. It's not a task of a day; it's a journey that has passed from many births. Your energy has been transformed, modelled, diminished and levitated over timeless centuries and will go on until you find the code to liberate it and merge it with the light.

Your Kali will guide you, give you indications, trigger a thought, spark an idea, but, ultimately, it's your energy that must work to find its home.

Let your self-worth be defined by your mind, your soul. She is your Kali; you are her. Embrace her and gradually let her show you the true worth of your soul.

Form is an illusion. Energy is real.

Merging

ONENESS

Kali dances with unbounded passion,
She sings with pride; break the illusion of wrong and right,
Like melting moon her aura glows with light.
There is no wall, conjoin with my spirit today,
Slay your demons of ignorance,
Merge in the novel knowing, a new day.
You are me and I am you,
When were we ever apart?
Let the flickering light turn into a ball of fire,
Kali, I rest today all my desires.

–Ekta

FINDING THE BALANCE

Kali is active. She is dancing in full form. Her eyes are fierce and wet with crucifying pain, slaying her own creation. She is inviting women to join her rhythm, her dance of creation. "This is not destruction," she screams with ecstasy. "This is restoration." When women disrespect their truest power, disharmony is first created at home and then it extends to the outer world. For harmony to be restored, women have to embrace their innate nature of creation, meditate on their power of nurturing and merge with the nature. The seed of balance will rise from her own core.

While the world frantically looks for a cure outside, women must connect to their inner warrior and expand on the energy that exudes from her navel. Every woman holds the power to restore the imbalance if she taps into the dormant Shiv (potent energy) within her, and after deep meditation, opens the womb of life from within. She will then give birth to faith, to peace, to love, to courage and to wisdom. She will dance the same rhythm as Kali, for she will know that the vessel that carries her energy is nature itself. Once she learns to honour her inner nature, she will be free of the fear of losing what was never hers.

It's time that nature reminds the world that it is she that holds the creation with love.

Women must join in mass, connect as a tribe and offer the world love, compassion and light. The restoration will happen first within, then at home and expand to the world. *Kali is asking women to join her dance of creation and pray to mother nature with love and passion, pray with gratitude and vow to restore her honour.* Women must accept the chaos and continually radiate and expand her energy to join other women as warriors of light—enlightened, awakened and welcoming the restoration to take the world to the next level of awakening, to the age of Kali.

- ONENESS -

EMBRACING RELATIONSHIPS

Every woman knows that every relationship in her life will go through momentous cycles of life and death, randomness and uniformity, passion and pain, strength and despair. She will know that this is the essence of the energy of that relationship. Her Kali will guide her to trust her instincts and know when to end or elongate a certain relationship. To love, one must not only be strong but also wise. Strength comes from spirit and wisdom comes from experience.

Every relationship has a life and a purpose. To think that what's momentary is an infinite bond is to fool ourselves. When you meet someone, what merges and what interacts is the energy. Sometimes we may be depleted in certain energy, and that results in a stagnation and lack of interest in life. The moment a different energy interacts with us, our own energy finds its spark and ignites life again. What should become the trigger to replenish and further enhance the self-sustained energy, sadly for some, becomes a weakness and emotional dependency, especially women.

Remember that sometimes in our journey, we meet catalysts who help us find our direction. You may relish their energy for a while but they are not meant to stay forever. Such catalysts suddenly enter your life in an instant and, similarly, abruptly leave your domain. Their moment and time in your life are like a flash of lightning: intense, overpowering and brief. Don't hold on to the sorrow of the end of such a relationship. The purpose has been fulfilled and the universe is asking you to move on with the awakened rekindled wisdom. Just as you found a catalyst in your life to help you elevate your energy, you yourself have been in past and will be in future, the catalyst energy on someone's life. These energies interact as friends, workmates, sisters, strangers—the list is endless. Kali reminds us women that the life game is all about exchanging energies and wisdom. Let go of what is no longer nourishing your soul and move ahead, dancing with the flow.

Everyone we meet is a reflection of our own self. This world is like a mirror. It reflects our own self in others. We have to learn to live through each trait and desire within us to be able to understand who we truly are.

As the onion has multiple layers, so is our soul covered with layers of personalities, desires and experiences. To reach the deepest core, we must peel the layers one at a time. This is manifested through people we meet on our journey. Each person reflects a speck of our personality. We are attracted to some, some we loath, from some we learn, from some we hide.

Kali laughs as she witnesses this drama endlessly with utmost patience. She reminds us again that every soul we meet will remind us of something that our soul is searching for. It will give us the opportunity to indulge in that energy and live it through the experiences we have with the other soul. Once that is done, we will be given a choice to either embrace it and move on or be stuck in a timeless journey of denial and hate, only to meet that soul again and live through the same experiences again, until we learn to accept. For a woman to truly embrace her inner Kali, she must first accept the role of the other souls in her timeless journey.

Do not let ignorance become your entity; let acceptance be the trigger that leads to wisdom and knowledge. Whoever comes in to your life, in whatever form, of love or hate, is there to release you and help you peel away a superficial layer of self. That soul is the manifestation of your inner denial, your desires and your subconscious experiences.

Women, being emotional by nature, must evoke their higher self to guide them at times when their soul feels emotionally vulnerable. She will then be able to comprehend the true purpose of the outward drama. She will learn to let go of enslavements of spiteful love and accept those that challenge her compassion. She will understand that every soul has a purpose in her life same as she has in theirs. Only when she detaches from the endless inner dilemma, will she be able to release herself and the other soul.

Your inner Kali is your true essence, the one that you are, the one who is the fragrance of your soul. She will manifest in many forms and energies, until you learn to embrace every form with love and compassion.

JOINING THE TRIBE

The current energy game is compelling each woman to question her place in this world, to analyse her priorities, to understand what is needed and what is damaging her soul. She is more aware of her emotions, she is feeling the power within her, she is connecting to the universe silently in the chaos of life. This is because the age of Kali is dawning upon the human race . Women are the closest to nature, as they themselves are the fertile ground of life. This gives them more sensitivity towards the change in energy shifts. The era of Kali is now giving the women a chance to liberate from past pains of many births, to awaken to a new consciousness where she defines her life purpose and comprehends the mystical forces with her own innate wisdom. Many women will feel vulnerable at such times of awakening. Their souls will guide them to release past pain to move to a higher level of consciousness. Do not fear the energy that makes you emotional, angry or irritable. Let it flow in and wash out the toxins, clear away the blockages and make room for wisdom and light.

Trust your Kali as she calls your energy to enter her tribe. Merge into her darkness to find your true light. Kali will guide you to find the answers that lie within your soul.

- MOMENT -

THE KALI MOMENT

A single moment can be a catalyst for the complete transformation of a life. Never underestimate the power of a single moment, a meeting or an idea that was a result of your intuition. A small thought can initiate a stalled journey, the one that can change the direction of life instantly. That one fleeting moment, the one that lasts for a few seconds, but in those illuminated minutes you experience a divine joy, a sense of relief and anxiety, an adrenaline rush akin to skydiving. That one moment of oneness and unison with the universe is the moment you decide to hush all the noises and hear the voice that has been singing a melody you are lured to follow. That one moment when you let your inner liberated self guide you. You surrender with love and without doubt you follow the words that your soul already knew. That one moment when holding on to your intuition, you follow a trail in darkness, believing that you will be guided constantly. That is the moment that will eventually become a blueprint and trigger for a colossal transformation. It could be so trivial that you let it pass as a coincidence but doing so will deepen the illusion of the ceiling and devoid you of the chance to open a new portal of knowledge and opportunities; knowledge that leads to knowing and knowing that leads to spiritual empowerment.

We don't see it but that moment of trust in intuition is what creates a ripple that gives rise to the storm, which ultimately becomes the force that breaks the ceiling and lets the answers flow.

Spiritual experiences are the real experiences of the soul. They are hard to comprehend but when looked through the inner eye, they become lucid and absolute bliss. These experiences are stepping stones to souls' real journey, the canvas of their journey and the anchor of faith. I believe that women are far more attuned to experience a spiritual jolt in life: a moment that shakes the deepest core of their existence and brings them face to face with their inner warrior woman, their Kali.

Either you have already experienced the Kali moment or your life is leading you towards one. Without a doubt, each one of us have or will soon face that moment. If you are already on your spiritual quest or have chosen the road less travelled, think, what was that one moment, that first moment that initiated a series of events leading to the bigger picture? We may experience many moments of awakening in our life but some decisions leave a lasting imprint. Think back to that one moment which led you to a turbulent, emotional rollercoaster of a journey, but that's one journey that you would

- MOMENT -

never want to erase from your life. It was worth it because the person you became after that is who you really are. It allowed you to take off the mask! What was the moment which restored your faith in yourself, made you feel alive or helped you regain your trust in intuition?

It could be any one of these situations:
1. That moment when you trusted your instincts and refused to succumb to societal norms.
2. That moment when you said no to unintended sarcasm and walked out of the door without regret.
3. That moment when you decided to respect your choices.

You don't arrive at a Kali moment instantly. Our soul recognises the knock on the door that has always just been there. You have been tempted time and again to open it but stepped back in fear of the unknown. Every time you felt a nudge in your heart that something was not right, you could hear the soft knock getting louder and stronger. It's not a usual knock, rather it has a distant melody to it; the one that you have maybe heard in your dreams sometimes. That door is luminous and large with a symbolic huge red circular and mystical dot. "Why red?" you may ask. Because red is the colour of our foundation. It's the colour of fire, ecstasy, life, rage and strength.

- MOMENT -

The colour of our base chakra, red symbolises the power we hold in our soul. It initiates the urge and thought of creating a momentum in the static state of life.

The stronger your urge grows to open the door, the brighter the dot illuminates. Then, one day you think it is the time. A surge of emotions arises, from fear, doubt, denial, anxiety, excitement, joy, depression to that one moment when all emotions merge into just one – surrender. That phase of denial may last for years or for months, but when you surrender with full faith to the universal energy, that is the time when you are ready to walk and open that door. The energy that is constantly knocking on the other side of the door is your own warrior archetype –your Kali. *She is your own fearless reflection, waiting with patience for you to trust her and let her lead your life.* She is hoping that you will submerge your fears and doubts in her darkness so she may guide you towards the light. She is you and you are her.

Life is a journey from wherever you are now to that door; that door with a red dot that is waiting to be opened. A journey from your current empowered self to your highest empowered psychic state: your Kali.

- MOMENT -

MY KALI MOMENT

As far as I can remember, I have always had a heightened sixth sense. I could, even as a child, dream of events beforehand and make random predictions that became true. For a long time, I thought that this was absolutely normal, but as I grew, I gradually realised that this was not how the world worked. I particularly remember the look of surprise on my mother's face when my nursery teacher at Pune, a small town in India, asked her about our plans to move to a different town. Apparently, I had announced with conviction that this would be my last week at that school because my dad had been posted to New Delhi and we had to leave immediately. My mother brushed it off as my imagination, but when we arrived home, my dad called to say that we were to move to New Delhi soon, as he had been posted there.

My father is a retired Army officer, which meant that during my growing years we were posted to a new city every two years. I have many times not just dreamt of the house that we would live in or the place and date of posting; I have also seen the people that we would meet on the way, quite to precision.

As I started growing, my spiritual gifts expanded as well. I sometimes saw flashes of light, souls, and often felt a strange warm energy pass through me. Visions became more detailed and vivid, but one incident completely surpassed any spiritual experience that I ever had.

I had just turned 20 when I realised that every morning at about 5am I would hear a continuous chatter of people in my sleep. I was probably in a half sleep state because I do remember looking at my room with blurry eyes and trying to cover my ears to mitigate the clamour. This was the time when my parents went for their morning walk and I was alone in our modest three-bedroom apartment. The noise would usually fade away after about ten minutes, but those screams and chatter remained with me all through the day. I was working as a graphic designer in an advertising agency and this bizarre experience was greatly impacting my output at work. After about one week, I confided to my mother, who very calmly asked me to surrender this situation to the universe.

The following night, I asked my angels to help me. It was early morning when I felt a strange force behind me. Turning around lazily, I was startled to see an angelic energy in front of me; a lady in black attire was sitting right next to me! I suddenly realised that I was sitting upright and yet strangely my body was lying calmly on the bed. I felt both distant and oddly connected to it. The angelic lady felt familiar, as if she has been travelling with me through many lifetimes. I almost felt that she was the force and magic behind every vision and dream that I had since childhood. We were not speaking, yet there was an effortless conversation taking place between us. Her presence was enigmatic and loving. She permitted me gently to ask for a blessing. My mind was baffled – what did I really want? How can a lifetime of wishes be accumulated in a moment? I was not prepared, but my soul certainly was. I asked for the boon to be graced with the insight to make the right decision every time I face a crossroad. This boon which came from the deepest core of my soul has been my anchor and biggest blessing to date. As I sat mesmerised by her beauty and aura, she reached her glowing hand towards me and touched my forehead gently. A chill ran through my veins , and the very next moment I was fully awake and reconnected to my body.

That was the first time my guardian angel, my Kali, came to me and initiated my journey with her. Love and marriage brought me to London, which again was a vision come true. A voice whispered a name in my ears the moment I woke up one morning 17 years back. Later that day, in an absolutely unplanned manner, I spoke to my would-be husband for the first time on the phone. I was shocked when I heard his name; it was the same name whispered in my ears that morning by an unknown force. In an instant I knew that this was the man I would marry. A few months prior to meeting him, visions of living in a distant place had been recurring in my dreams and I was somehow sure that I would soon be uprooted from my birth country. We got married three months later and, bizarrely, I moved to London after just ten days of the wedding. Needless to say, my house was in a valley that had been showing its glimpses in my dreams.

London was welcoming and a home away from home. After the vision of Kali, my quest for spiritual wisdom kept escalating with passing years. I read, researched and gradually found that my visions were being channelised through words. My desire to share my passion for positive thinking led me to approach a community radio station who very generously trained me, and within a month I was running my solo show, Go Positive, on the radio.

Considering that my words and voice had found a platform to inspire, I thought that my spiritual quest and learning had been fulfilled. I was channeling her words through short messages and had found my Kali, waiting for me at the other side of the door. What more was left? That thought was my biggest mistake. Spiritual journey is not for the weak-hearted. The real test begins the moment you think you have opened the door. It is in those few steps away from the door when you are tested to your limits. When you believe you have connected to the universal energies, almost as an irony, they disconnect from you instantly to test your surrender and sometimes to save you from spiritual ego. My misconception was also broken and I was thrown into the most turbulent eight years of my life.

There came a time when everything went against my way. Life started showing an exact opposite of what I had been used to. I experienced resentment, saw darker shades of human nature and my entrepreneurial ventures kept failing. This conflict was confusing my perception. I felt miserable, broken and shattered. My faith wavered and I started doubting my visions. I hated myself for being so naïve and believing in random dreams that could have been coincidences. Self-pity engulfed my mind completely. I was misunderstood and misjudged, not by others but by my own thoughts. My loved ones watched me in despair, as so did I.

One night, after going through years of fighting hard luck, my hopes shattered and I lay down my weapons to surrender to the force that had always guided me. Gathering the broken pieces, with full faith in my heart, I asked my angel to guide and show me the lesson that I was meant to learn through this challenging time. Perhaps, I had asked the right question that night. My angel, my Kali, came to me in my dreams. She was dressed in black and gold. Her familiar soothing smile reassured me that she had always been by my side. In one instance, I realised that I was never really alone. The struggles, the hardships, the failures that felt so painful were, in reality, a master plan of the universe to awaken me to a new truth. The whole scene had been created in my life just to give momentum to my stalled spiritual journey. I was not a nobody; I was part of the universe. Had I not gone through the struggles that I did, I would have never really pushed myself to surrender with the intensity of faith that I had done that night. *The dark night of my life had shown me the light that was always within me.* The vision of Kali shook my entire being. Her energy was calling me to know and embrace her loving yet ferocious enigma. I was scared, apprehensive and excited.

Gradually, I started reading about her. The more I learnt, the more I liberated. I started taking steps towards rebuilding my life. Kali guided me as a friend and a guru in this process. That moment of absolute surrender was my Kali moment.

- MOMENT -

A NEW BEGINNING

Kali questions all women who believe in self-power. Her query is strange and healing as she silently inspires them to dig deep and tell her what empowerment implies. "What is the point that will inspire a woman to break from her current life into a life she weaves silently? What is the drama that will finally jolt her in panic to find her own wings? What are the words that will bring out the cry of her inner voice and make her search for the Kali that is hidden beneath mystic layers of deception and illusion?"

"Who is Kali?" Kali mocks again. "Just words that impress or the life that's alive."

Kali is power, the life, the force that animates the static and the voice that sings in freedom. She is the mistress of the dark, yet she illuminates light. Kali is your soul sister, a fellow traveller of many births. She is the voice that you are tempted to listen to. She is the warrior woman within you, waiting to be unveiled. May you find your Kali soon.

Join my tribe

Connect with me via my blog, www.thekalimoment.com, or send me an email at thevoiceofkali@gmail.com.

Share your transformational stories with me? When did you reach your Kali moment? How was your journey? Are you going through a phase of awakening? Is your inner warrior woman trying to communicate with you? Tell me how this book reached you. Has the book answered your questions? Do you wish to know more? Have you found guidance and inspiration through this book?

Much love,
Ekta Bajaj

Instagram: @voice_of_kali
Twitter: @Ektabajaj
Facebook: @voiceofkalispeaks